HAPPY TIME

(On S'Amuse Au Piano)

T0048231

by ALEXANDRE TANSMAN

Contents

ISBN 978-0-7935-2304-7

HAL•LEONARD®
CORPORATION
7777 W. BLUEMOUND RD. P.O. BOX 13819 MILWAUKEE, WI 53213

Visit Hal Leonard Online at
www.halleonard.com

Both Ways   Échanges

ALEXANDRE TANSMAN

Moderato

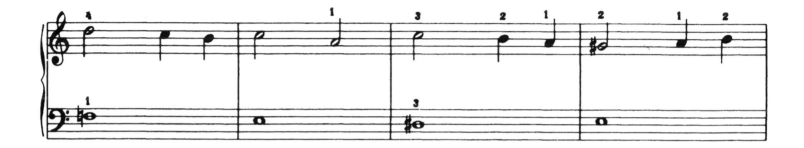

Little Gavotte   Petite Gavotte

ALEXANDRE TANSMAN

Waltzing   En Valsant

ALEXANDRE TANSMAN

Common Tones   Notes Communes

ALEXANDRE TANSMAN

Arabia   Arabie

ALEXANDRE   TANSMAN

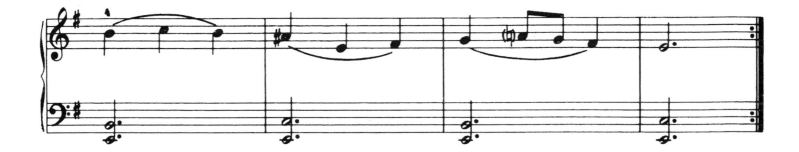

Frolic   Espièglerie

ALEXANDRE TANSMAN

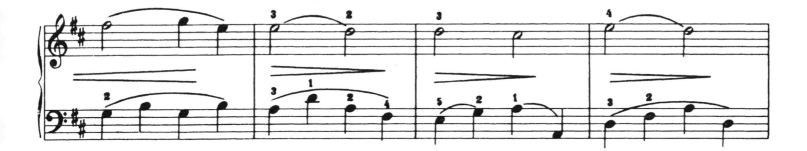

Shadow   Ombre

ALEXANDRE   TANSMAN

Sailors' Dance   Danse des Matelots

ALEXANDRE TANSMAN

Allegro con moto

Lullaby   Chant à bercer

ALEXANDRE TANSMAN

Reflections   Réflexions

ALEXANDRE TANSMAN

Little Stroll   Petite Promenade

ALEXANDRE TANSMAN

Melody Mélodie

Moderato

ALEXANDRE TANSMAN

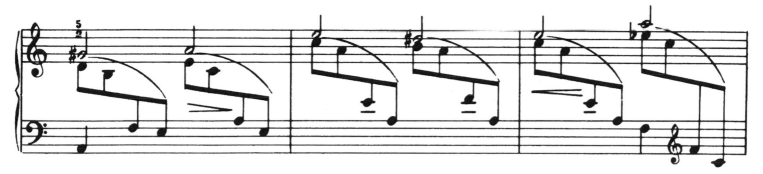

Popular Air Air populaire

ALEXANDRE TANSMAN

Dreams Rêves

ALEXANDRE TANSMAN

Obsession   Rengaine

ALEXANDRE TANSMAN